THIS IS THE WORLD THAT GOD BUILT

THIS IS THE WORLD THAT GOD BUILT

By Amy Nichols
Illustrated by Ekaterina Ilina

Wipf & Stock
An Imprint of Wipf and Stock Publishers
199 W. 8th Ave., Suite 3
Eugene, OR 97401
www.wipfandstock.com
PAPERBACK ISBN: 978-1-7252-5781-8
HARDCOVER ISBN: 978-1-7252-5782-5
EBOOK ISBN: 978-1-7252-5783-2
Manufactured in the U.S.A.

Dedicated to Ben and Lily
When life gets hard (and it will) and things seem impossible,
just look around at all the beautiful and amazing wonders
of Creation and be assured that nothing
is impossible for God!
Love Mom.

DAY 1

This is the world that God built.
This is the darkness that covered the deep
In the world that God built.

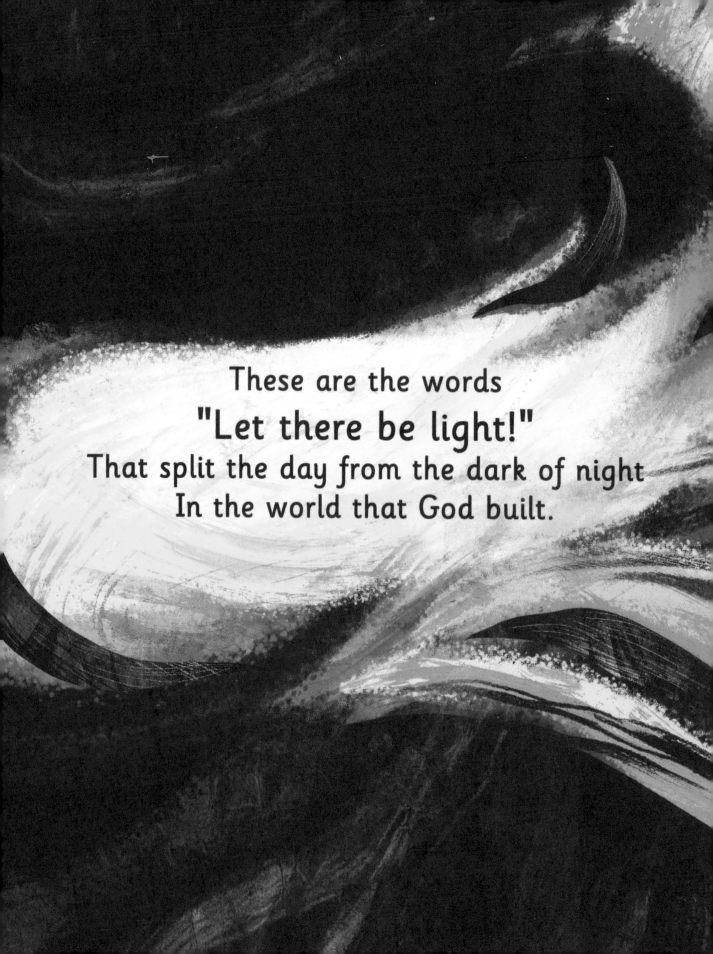

These are the words
"Let there be light!"
That split the day from the dark of night
In the world that God built.

DAY 2

These are the waters, low and high
Divided into sea and sky
After the words "Let there be light!"
Split the day from the dark of night
In the world that God built.

DAY 3

This is the land gathered to lie
Among the seas, below the sky
After the words "Let there be light!"
Split the day from the dark of night
In the world that God built.

These are the mountains high,
Oceans deep and deserts dry
That shape the land gathered to lie
Among the seas, below the sky
After the words "Let there be light!"
Split the day from the dark of night
In the world that God built.

These are the plants and trees that grow
On mountain tops and valleys low
That shape the land gathered to lie
Among the seas, below the sky
After the words "Let there be light!"
Split the day from the dark of night
In the world that God built.

DAY 4

This is the sun that beams bright
And the stars and moon that light the night
Above the plants and trees that grow
On mountain tops and valleys low
That shape the land gathered to lie
Among the seas, below the sky
After the words "Let there be light!"
Split the day from the dark of night
In the world that God built.

DAY 5

These are the creatures of sky and sea
From giant whale to tiny bee
Under the sun that beams bright
And the stars and moon that light the night
Above the plants and trees that grow
On mountain tops and valleys low
That shape the land gathered to lie
Among the seas, below the sky
After the words "Let there be light!"
Split the day from the dark of night
In the world that God built.

DAY 6

These are the animals, wild and tame
That roam the earth's diverse terrain
With the creatures of sky and sea
From giant whale to tiny bee
Under the sun that beams bright
And the stars and moon that light the night
Above the plants and trees that grow
On mountain tops and valleys low
That shape the land gathered to lie
Among the seas, below the sky
After the words "Let there be light!"
Split the day from the dark of night
In the world that God built.

This is man formed of image divine
To care for all of God's design
Every animal, wild and tame
That roam the earth's diverse terrain
With the creatures of sky and sea
From giant whale to tiny bee
Under the sun that beams bright
And the stars and moon that light the night
Above the plants and trees that grow
On mountain tops and valleys low
That shape the land gathered to lie
Among the seas, below the sky
After the words "Let there be light!"
Split the day from the dark of night
In the world that God built.

This is woman of man's rib to be
A helper, friend, and wife for thee,
Man formed of image divine
To care for all of God's design,
Every animal, wild and tame
That roam the earth's diverse terrain
With the creatures of sky and sea
From giant whale to tiny bee
Under the sun that beams bright
And the stars and moon that light the night
Above the plants and trees that grow
On mountain tops and valleys low
That shape the land gathered to lie
Among the seas, below the sky
After the words "Let there be light!"
Split the day from the dark of night
In the world that God built.

This is the beautiful world we see
A gift from God to you and me
From woman of man's rib to be
A helper, friend, and wife for thee,
Man formed of image divine
To care for all of God's design,
Every animal, wild and tame
That roam the earth's diverse terrain
With the creatures of sky and sea
From giant whale to tiny bee
Under the sun that beams bright
And the stars and moon that light the night
Above the plants and trees that grow
On mountain tops and valleys low
That shape the land gathered to lie
Among the seas, below the sky
After the words "Let there be light!"
Split the day from the dark of night
In the world that God built.

DAY 7

This is the world that God built.
This is the day, holy and blessed
When God sat back to admire and rest.
All the beautiful world we see
Is a gift from God to you and me.

Creation Story Bible Verse Excerpts (New International Version)

Day One

Genesis 1:1, In the beginning God created the heavens and the earth.

Genesis 1:2, Now the earth was formless and empty, darkness was over the surface of the deep, and the Spirit of God was hovering over the waters.

Genesis 1:3, And God said, "Let there be light," and there was light.

Genesis 1:4, God saw that the light was good, and he separated the light from the darkness.

Genesis 1:5, God called the light "day," and the darkness he called "night."

Day Two

Genesis 1:6, And God said, "Let there be a vault between the waters to separate water from water."

Genesis 1:8, God called the vault "sky."

Day Three

Genesis 1:9, And God said, "Let the water under the sky be gathered to one place, and let dry ground appear."

Genesis 1:10, God called the dry ground "land," and the gathered waters he called "seas."

Genesis 1:11, Then God said, "Let the land produce vegetation: seed-bearing plants and trees on the land that bear fruit with seed in it, according to their various kinds."

Day Four

Genesis 1:14, And God said, "Let there be lights in the vault of the sky to separate the day from the night, and let them serve as signs to mark sacred times, and days and years."

Genesis 1:15, and let them be lights in the vault of the sky to give light on the earth."

Day Five

Genesis 1:20, And God said, "Let the water teem with living creatures, and let birds fly above the earth across the vault of the sky."

Day Six

Genesis 1:24, And God said, "Let the land produce living creatures according to their kinds: the livestock, the creatures that move along the ground, and the wild animals, each according to its kind."

Genesis 1:26, Then God said, "Let us make mankind in our image, in our likeness, so that they may rule over the fish in the sea and the birds in the sky, over the livestock and all the wild animals, and over all the creatures that move along the ground."

Genesis 2:18, The LORD God said, "It is not good for the man to be alone. I will make a helper suitable for him."

Genesis 2:21, So the LORD God caused the man to fall into a deep sleep; and while he was sleeping, he took one of the man's ribs and then closed up the place with flesh.

Genesis 2:22, Then the LORD God made a woman from the rib he had taken out of the man, and he brought her to the man.

Day Seven

Genesis 2:2, By the seventh day God had finished the work he had been doing; so on the seventh day he rested from all his work.

Genesis 2:3, Then God blessed the seventh day and made it holy, because on it he rested from all the work of creating that he had done.